ADOLF
HITLER

Essential Lives

ADOLF HITLER

GERMAN DICTATOR

by Sue Vander Hook

Content Consultant:
Arnold Krammer, PhD
professor, Texas A&M University

ABDO
Publishing Company

CREDITS

Published by ABDO Publishing Company, 8000 West 78th Street, Edina, Minnesota 55439. Copyright © 2011 by Abdo Consulting Group, Inc. International copyrights reserved in all countries. No part of this book may be reproduced in any form without written permission from the publisher. The Essential Library™ is a trademark and logo of ABDO Publishing Company.

Printed in the United States of America,
North Mankato, Minnesota
112010
012011

 THIS BOOK CONTAINS AT LEAST 10% RECYCLED MATERIALS.

Editor: Rebecca Rowell
Copy Editor: David Johnstone
Interior Design and Production: Marie Tupy
Cover Design: Kazuko Collins

Library of Congress Cataloging-in-Publication Data
Vander Hook, Sue, 1949-
  Adolf Hitler : German dictator / By Sue Vander Hook.
    p. cm. -- (Essential lives)
  Includes bibliographical references.
  ISBN 978-1-61714-781-4
  1. Hitler, Adolf, 1889-1945--Juvenile literature. 2. Heads of state--Germany--Biography--Juvenile literature. 3. Germany--History--1933-1945--Juvenile literature. 4. National socialism--Juvenile literature. I. Title.
  DD247.H5V37 2011
  943.086092--dc22
  [B]
                                        2010041262

TABLE OF CONTENTS

*The bomb Stauffenberg left at Wolf's Lair caused considerable damage
to the room where Hitler had been meeting with staff members.*

THE WOLF'S LAIR

Adolf Hitler leaned far over the heavy oak conference table to look closely at a map. It was July 20, 1944, and Germany's dictator was worried. He was afraid he might be losing this war that had come to be called World

War II. Some of Hitler's top military officers were with him that day at Wolfsschanze. German for "wolf's lair," Wolfsschanze was Hitler's secret military site located in a secluded wooded area of East Prussia (now Poland). It was one of several German military headquarters where Hitler and his generals often strategized about the war.

Standing to Hitler's right was Lieutenant General Adolf Heusinger. He was telling Hitler the grim details of Germany's dire situation. During the conversation, Lieutenant Colonel Claus von Stauffenberg approached the table on Heusinger's right. He quietly placed a brown briefcase underneath the table just six feet (1.8 m) from Hitler. Then, he slipped out of the room, walked quickly down a long hallway, and exited the building.

Unknown to Stauffenberg, Heusinger's aide, Colonel Heinz Brandt, walked up to the table and moved the briefcase to get a closer look at the map. Although he moved it only a small distance, his act would have huge consequences.

DISASTER AT WOLFSSCHANZE

At 12:42 p.m., Heusinger said to Hitler, "Unless at long last the army group is withdrawn from

Peipus, a catastrophe . . . ."[1] At that moment, an explosion blew up the conference room. Windows shattered, wood splinters and plaster fell from the ceiling, and the floor buckled. Flames shot up all around, and the room filled with smoke. Hitler and his field marshal headed hastily for the door. Hitler's uniform was in shreds and his face was black with ashes. His hair was scorched, and more than 200 wood splinters pierced his legs. Both men made their way down the long corridor, out the door, and into Hitler's private bunker.

Inside the conference room, German officers staggered from their injuries. All but one had punctured eardrums, many were bleeding, and four would die within days from their wounds. Ironically, one of the fatalities would be Colonel Brandt, the officer who had moved the bomb-filled briefcase. He had saved Hitler's life and lost his own.

Within minutes, medical personnel were on the scene. Dr. Hanskarl von Hasselbach, one of Hitler's personal physicians, placed a sling on Hitler's badly sprained elbow, checked his heart, and gave him an injection. All the while, a talkative Hitler blamed foreign workers at a nearby construction site for the bomb and called them cowards. He repeated ecstatically, "Think of it. Nothing has happened to me. Just think of it."[2] With a smile, he reminded three of his secretaries, "Well, my ladies, . . . once again everything turned out well for me. More proof that Fate has selected me for my mission. Otherwise I wouldn't be alive."[3]

STAUFFENBERG FLEES

Stauffenberg did not wait to see the results of the bombing. He and his adjutant, or assistant, bluffed their way through two security gates and then boarded a plane to Berlin, Germany. Three hours later, the two men met up with

The Wolf's Lair

Hitler's Wolfsschanze was built in 1940 in what was then East Prussia as a strategic planning center for the German leader and his military aides. The complex included ten bunkers shielded by steel-reinforced concrete. The buildings were concealed by bushes, grass, and artificial trees on the rooftops. From the air, the complex blended in with the surrounding forest.

As many as 2,000 people lived at the complex during the height of the war. The outer area was protected by land mines and special military guards called the Führer's Armored Battalion. They were heavily armed with anti-aircraft weapons and tanks. A nearby airfield and railroad provided quick access to, and swift retreat from, the site.

When at Wolfsschanze, Hitler began his day at about 9:00 a.m. by walking his dog. At about 10:30, Hitler read his mail. At noon, he attended military briefings, followed by a long lunch at 2:00 p.m. and more meetings. He ate a vegetarian dinner at 7:30 p.m. and then reviewed films of the war. Sometimes, Hitler and his staff listened to records. His favorite music included Beethoven symphonies, Wagner operas, and traditional German songs. Typically, at the end of the evening, Hitler delivered a motivating speech to his staff.

their coconspirators—a group of Germans who had long been trying to assassinate Hitler and topple his Nazi regime.

The group did not know yet if the bomb had killed Hitler, but Stauffenberg was convinced that no one could have survived the fiery blast. He immediately encouraged other members of the German resistance to carry out the next phase of their plan—code named "Valkyrie"—to overthrow the entire Nazi leadership. But that evening, Hitler's own voice on the radio changed their plan.

Stauffenberg now knew Hitler was still alive. And Hitler knew Stauffenberg was responsible for his attempted assassination. Someone remembered seeing Stauffenberg put the briefcase under the table. Someone else told Hitler about Stauffenberg's hasty retreat to Berlin. Hitler ordered Stauffenberg's arrest.

That night, Nazi officers in Berlin quickly tracked down Stauffenberg and three of his coconspirators. Stauffenberg was wounded after a brief shoot-out, which was followed by an impromptu trial and court

Operation Valkyrie

Valkyrie is a word from German and Old Norse meaning "chooser of the slain." In Norse mythology, Valkyries swooped over battlefields and conveyed dead warriors to Valhalla. German composer Richard Wagner named one of his dramatic operas *The Valkyrie*. The relevance of the Valkyries to the plot is anybody's guess.

On July 20, 2009, in Berlin, German soldiers marched in front of the Reichstag, which houses the German parliament. The soldiers took their oath, commemorating the sixty-fifth anniversary of Stauffenberg's failed assault on Hitler.

martial. At 12:30 a.m. on July 21, 1944, the four rebels were shot and killed by a Nazi firing squad. The executions took place in the inner courtyard of the huge Army High Command, or headquarters, building on Bendlerstrasse in Berlin, where many of the conspirators had their offices. Stauffenberg was the last to be shot. When the firing squad was ordered to shoot, he shouted, "Long live our sacred Germany!"[4] Then, he died.

"A Sign from Providence"

At 1:00 a.m., Hitler was on the air again, broadcasting on state radio the news of the failed assassination attempt. Hitler told his listeners,

> *I was spared a fate which held no horror for me, but would have had terrible consequences for the German people. I see in it a sign from Providence that I must, and therefore shall, continue my work.*[5]

Hermann Göring, one of Hitler's top military leaders, then announced that those responsible for the assassination attempt had either committed suicide or been shot.

When Hitler returned to his bunker, he was jubilant. He had miraculously escaped death once again and foiled his opponents' plot to kill him.

Soldiers had been fighting in World War II since 1939. Hitler would continue his reign of terror, elude capture, postpone defeat, and murder millions before the world was finally rid of one of the greatest mass murderers and cruel dictators of all time.

HIER STARBEN
FÜR
DEUTSCHLAND
AM 20.JULI 1944

GENERALOBERST LUDWIG BECK
GENERAL DER INFANTERIE FRIEDRICH OLBRICHT
OBERST CLAUS GRAF SCHENK VON STAUFFENBERG
OBERST ALBRECHT RITTER MERTZ VON QUIRNHEIM
OBERLEUTNANT WERNER VON HAEFTEN

An honor guard stands by a plaque commemorating the execution of
Stauffenberg and others at Berlin's German Resistance Memorial Center.

Austria is known for its beautiful landscape, including mountains.

Spoiled and Thrashed

On April 20, 1889, in Braunau am Inn in Austria-Hungary, a baby boy was born to Klara Pölzl Hitler and Alois Hitler. They named him Adolf. He was their fourth and only living child. The Hitlers had been married for five years but had already suffered the loss of three children. One died at birth, and two died as toddlers after contracting diphtheria. Klara was terrified her new baby boy would also die.

Klara focused all her love and attention on Adolf. Two older children from Alois's previous marriage also lived in the Hitler household. Klara mostly ignored them, keeping constant watch on Adolf. She claimed he was sickly and needed her attention. Klara's lavish love and overprotectiveness resulted in a spoiled child who got everything he wanted.

Adolf's father was strict, demanding, and unapproachable. He was known in the community for his unpredictable temper and at home for his stern, authoritative discipline. Alois was especially harsh with Adolf and beat him regularly. Klara would often listen to the thrashings, helpless against the wrath of her husband.

MANY MOVES AND SCHOOL

In 1894, when Adolf was five years old, his father was promoted to a respectable government position as customs inspector in Linz, Austria.

Klara and Alois Hitler

Klara Pölzl was 23 years younger than her husband, Alois Hitler. She was Alois's third wife. His first two wives died. Klara and Alois were probably second cousins. Since they were so closely related, they had to get special permission from the Vatican, the seat of the Catholic Church, to get married.

He lived and worked in Linz by himself for a year. The family was on its own.

While Alois was in Linz, Klara gave birth to another son, Edmund. Her attention was on the new baby, and with Alois gone, Adolf became more independent. He played cowboys and Indians by himself for hours and invented his own war games. He always made sure he had the last word with his mother. If he did not get his way, young Adolf threw a tantrum.

In 1895, Alois, now 58, retired from his government job.

Hitler's Last Name

The origin of Hitler's name is confusing. When his father was born in 1837, his name was Alois Schicklgruber. Alois's mother was 42-year-old Maria Schicklgruber. Alois's birth record included the notation "out of wedlock," and the space for the name of his father was blank.

When Alois was five years old, his mother married Johann Georg Hiedler. Seven years later, his mother died. Hiedler left and 12-year-old Alois grew up under the care of his uncle. By all accounts, Alois grew up in a good home. As a young teenager, Alois trained as an apprentice with a local cobbler, but then traveled to the capital, Vienna, to seek his fortune, joining the border police.

In 1876, Hiedler reappeared to notarize a statement that he was Alois's father in order to allow Alois to get a share of an inheritance. At the age of 39, Alois had his birth record legally altered. The blank space for his father's name was filled in with Georg Hitler, a common spelling of Hiedler his father had decided to use. Other spellings include Hüttler, Hittler, and Heitler. The name Schicklgruber was crossed out, and "out of wedlock" was replaced with "within wedlock." Alois Schicklgruber thus became Alois Hitler.

He purchased a small farm near the community of Fischlham, located approximately 30 miles (48 km) from Linz, which is near the border of Czechoslovakia (now the Czech Republic). There, he could pursue his beekeeping hobby. Once the family got settled, six-year-old Adolf started school. He was an average student, behaved well, and played outside after school with friends.

At home, however, tensions were rising. Since retiring, Alois was home most of the time, and there was a new baby in the family—a daughter named Paula, born in 1896. The farm was proving to be a financial burden, and Alois was constantly irritated with his children. In 1897, he sold the farm and moved his family to nearby Lambach, where Adolf attended another school. Adolf made good grades, but he was becoming "rather hard to handle," as one of his teachers explained.[1]

Adolf did not attend school in Lambach very long. In November 1898, his father moved the family again—to Leonding, a village outside Linz. Adolf liked that part of Austria and would always consider Linz his hometown. He was now in his third elementary school and made new friends once again. After school, he organized games of cops and robbers, cowboys and Indians, and war games in the open fields. But his life was about to change.

What Do You Want to Be?

In 1900, tragedy struck the Hitler household. Adolf's six-year-old brother, Edmund, died from the measles. Adolf's older stepbrother was no longer at home; he had left angry, with hard feelings toward his father, Alois. The atmosphere in the Hitler household was tense.

Eleven-year-old Adolf was ready for secondary school. In Austria, young Adolf could attend one of two types of secondary schools: *Realschule* or *Gymnasium*. Realschule, which Alois chose for his son, would provide Adolf with a practical education in science and technical studies. Gymnasium would have prepared Adolf for advanced academic study in the arts and was for more academically promising students. Alois thought Adolf should follow in his footsteps and work in a government office, a position that did not require a lot of education. Adolf disagreed.

"It was especially my brother Adolf, who challenged my father to extreme harshness and who got his sound thrashing every day. How often on the other hand did my mother caress him and try to obtain with her kindness, where the father could not succeed with harshness!"[2]

—Paula Hitler

Finally, when Adolf was 12, his father asked him what he wanted to be. An artist, Adolf told him, a painter. Adolf later recalled his father's response: "Artist, no, never as long as I live!"[3] Adolf became more determined to be an artist. He decided to stop studying and fail his courses. He thought that would make his father change his mind.

Death and Freedom

Adolf was angry. Once an active, happy, motivated child, he was now a stubborn adolescent. Father and son were in constant conflict. When Adolf was 13, his father collapsed suddenly in the tavern where he spent much of his time, and died. Most likely, the family, especially Adolf, did not grieve over his death.

Adolf did little schoolwork after his father died and continued to get failing grades. For a while, he attended boarding school in Steyr, about 50 miles (80 km) from Linz. His schoolwork improved there, but he detested school. When he was 16, Adolf pretended to be very ill and convinced his mother to let him drop out of school. Adolf spent hours alone in his room, drawing, painting, reading, and writing poetry. In the evenings, he often went to the opera

Paula Hitler

Adolf's sister, Paula, was his only full sibling to live to adulthood. At the end of World War II (1939–1945), she was arrested by US intelligence officers, questioned, and released. Paula returned to Vienna to work in an arts and crafts shop. On December 1, 1952, she moved to a small apartment near Berchtesgaden, Hitler's mountaintop retreat on the German-Austrian border. There, she lived in seclusion under the name of Mrs. Paula Wolf until her death on June 1, 1960, at the age of 64. She neither married nor had children. She was the only member of the immediate family to carry the name Hitler on her tombstone.

with his good friend August Kubizek. Adolf was obsessed with operas by Richard Wagner about German history, and he later described the composer's operas as a sort of mystical experience that gave him visions of his own future.

Life was easy for Adolf over the next two years. His mother, sister Paula, and Aunt Johanna tended to all his needs. He sat around dreaming of what it would be like to be a great artist. In 1906, when Adolf was 17, his mother paid for him to visit the art gallery in the Court Museum in Vienna, the capital and cultural center of Austria. When Adolf returned, his dream grew bigger—he wanted to study art at the Viennese Academy of Fine Arts. It would not be long before Adolf pursued his dream.

A painting of Klara Hitler, Adolf's mother

Chapter 3

Hitler headed to Vienna, Austria's capital, to seek his fortune.

ADRIFT IN VIENNA

When Hitler was 18 years old, he made plans to take the entrance examination at the Academy of Fine Arts in Vienna. Although his mother had become very ill with cancer, Hitler pursued his goal, which his mother supported.

In September 1907, Hitler left for Vienna with a large stack of his paintings and drawings. Acceptance into the school was difficult and based on the evaluation of his artwork by a committee of art professors over several days. He later wrote that he was "convinced that it would be child's play to pass the examination," since he had always been the best artist in all of his classrooms.[1]

After examining Hitler's art, academy officials did not accept him as a student. Their comments on his examination read, "Test drawing unsatisfactory. Few heads."[2] Hitler painted pictures of buildings, German street scenes, and rural pastures. On the rare occasions that people did appear in Hitler's paintings, few ever had any faces. The academy suggested Hitler attend architecture school instead. Hitler's self-confidence was shattered.

"A Dreadful Blow"

When Hitler returned home, he told no one of his failure to get into art school. Instead, he focused his full attention on caring for his mother, who was very near death. On December 21, 1907, Klara Pölzl Hitler died. Hitler called her passing "a dreadful blow."[3] He had lost the one person he had ever loved. He recalled later, "The death of my mother put a sudden end to all my high-flown plans. . . . I had honored my father, but my mother I had loved."[4]

In February 1908, Hitler returned to Vienna with some money and a desire to become an architect. He fell back into a life of idleness, self-pity, and loneliness. His good friend August Kubizek eventually joined him there, and they shared an apartment. Hitler had convinced Kubizek's parents their son should leave the family upholstery business and study music in Vienna, which is home to such renowned composers as Mozart and Beethoven. Kubizek was immediately accepted to the Vienna Conservatory, where he stood out as a gifted musical conductor.

Hitler was still convinced he was a good artist and applied a second time to the Academy of Fine Arts. He continued to live with Kubizek until the summer of 1908, when he was rejected by the academy a second

August Kubizek

After their time together in Vienna, Kubizek and Hitler lost contact until 1933, when Hitler became chancellor of Germany. When World War II ended, Kubizek collected keepsakes Hitler had given him and hid them in his basement. Because of his relationship with Hitler, Kubizek was subsequently interrogated and imprisoned for 16 months. US intelligence searched his home but did not find the Hitler mementos. In 1951, Kubizek wrote *Adolf Hitler, mein Jugendfreund* ("Adolf Hitler, My Young Friend"). Published in English with the title *The Young Hitler I Knew*, the book includes photos of Hitler in Vienna and pictures and paintings Hitler gave to Kubizek.

time and not even permitted to take the exam.
Hitler could not face his old friend in failure again.
Disgraced, devastated, and bitter, Hitler left his
apartment without telling Kubizek or anyone else.
Hitler sent postcards over the summer, but that was
the last contact he had with Kubizek. Hitler rented
a room elsewhere in Vienna for a while. But then he
walked out one night and never returned.

For the rest of 1908 Hitler lived comfortably,
relying on money from the government—an orphan
pension—his mother, and his aunt. But that soon
ran out. In 1909, Hitler became homeless, sleeping
in filthy shelters, hostels, parks, and sometimes by
the side of the street. He begged for money and
food, often going to a nearby convent for free soup.
Most of the time, he was hungry and tattered. He was
homeless and jobless—a drifter with long black hair
and a dark, unshaven face. He blamed everyone for
his failures. He later recalled his hard times: "The
uncertainty of earning my daily bread soon seemed
to me one of the darkest sides of my new life."[5]

Hitler's situation improved somewhat the
following year. In 1910, he met another drifter,
Reinhold Hanisch, who taught him how to find
food, shelter, and odd jobs. Together, they shoveled

snow and carried bags for passengers at the train station. When it was cold outside, they found refuge for a few hours in stores or hospitals. When Hitler fell into hopelessness and despair, Hanisch encouraged him to try to make money from his paintings. Hitler painted postcards of famous locations in Vienna, and Hanisch found buyers for them. The two men were making a small profit, so Hitler painted larger scenes. He completed about one painting a day, using money from his aunt to buy painting

---

The Männerheim

The Männerheim where Hitler stayed in Vienna was a large, modern building not far from the Danube River. German for "men's home," its 500 residents were homeless and looking for employment. For a fee, the home offered a private cubicle with a cot. The men had to vacate their space during the day. They could either buy their meals in the main-floor dining room or cook their own food on a stove in an adjacent kitchen. Next to the kitchen was a reading room with newspapers and magazines. Other rooms included a library and reading room, where some of them worked on their private businesses. This was the room where Hitler painted his postcards and Hanisch devised ways to market them.

In the basement were a laundry room and a long row of showers. There was also a cobbler, a tailor, and a barber. For a small fee, the men could rent private lockers in which they could store their personal possessions.

The Männerheim's director imposed strict rules on the men. Noise had to be kept to a minimum, and hard liquor was not allowed. The only games allowed were chess, checkers, and dominoes. All property had to be respected, and there was no standing on the beds.

supplies. The money they earned was enough for them to afford to stay in the Männerheim, a large home for single men.

ANTI-SEMITIC VIEWS

Politics was a favorite subject among the residents of the Männerheim. Hitler spent hours listening and debating with the other men who stayed there. He claimed it was at the men's home that he cultivated his anti-Semitic views. He came to believe Jews were cold-hearted, shameless, and calculating. Everywhere he looked, he thought he saw Jews in control—of the arts, the press, businesses, and trade unions. He now believed Jews "were not Germans of a special religion, but a people in themselves." He said, "Wherever I went, I began to see Jews, and the more I saw, the more sharply they became distinguished in my eyes from the rest of humanity."[6] Before long, Hitler hated them.

Jews in Hitler's Life

Customers for Hitler's postcards were Jewish merchants, and the Männerheim was actually funded by wealthy Jewish families to help those who needed a place to go while they got back on their feet. A close friend who helped with the art production business was also a Jew and Hitler was on friendly terms with him.

Hitler was also influenced by anti-Semitic pamphlets, magazines, and newspapers such as the *Deutsches Volksblatt*, which sold about 55,000 copies a day. The newspaper described Jews as "agents of decomposition and corruption."[7] He also read the *Ostara*, a cheap magazine that advocated superiority for a mythical tribe of blond-haired and blue-eyed white people—northern Aryans, as they were called. This idea was not new to him, but now it began to take deep root. Hitler imagined an entire nation of Aryans with no Jews or other people he deemed undesirable.

End of a Partnership

The partnership between Hitler and Hanisch ended in conflict when Hitler accused Hanisch of keeping all the proceeds from one of his paintings. Hanisch then began selling his own paintings and became Hitler's competitor. During the 1930s, as Hitler rose in power and notoriety, Hanisch sold his own artwork and claimed it had been painted by Hitler.

On May 24, 1913, the 24-year-old Hitler left Vienna. He was filled with anger, hatred, and bitterness. Those feelings would shape not only the man Hitler would become but also the world.

*While Hitler dreamed of becoming a professionally trained artist,
he made money selling his paintings on the streets of Vienna.*

Munich, Germany

WORLD WAR I SOLDIER

*H*itler was an Austrian citizen and was being sought by the Austrian military authorities for mandatory service. In May 1913, he slipped over the border into Germany without the proper stamp clearing him by the Austrian military.

Then in January 1914, the Austrian military tracked down the 24-year-old deserter and brought him back to Vienna. His letter of explanation to an Austrian official managed to keep Hitler out of prison. He was in such a shabby state, the official felt sorry for him and decided Hitler was being honest about his circumstances. He had applied for service years earlier and had not heard back from the military. The matter was dropped when Hitler actually failed the medical exam. He was found unfit and too weak for military service.

Hitler returned to Munich, where he made a meager living selling his paintings of Munich's landmarks. But his life changed dramatically on Sunday, June 28, 1914, when Germany and much of the rest of the world were thrown into the Great War, or World War I. That day, Archduke Franz Ferdinand, heir to the Austro-Hungarian Empire, was assassinated by Serbian extremists in Sarajevo, the capital of Bosnia (now Bosnia and Herzegovina). Ferdinand's wife, Sophie, was also killed.

Austria-Hungary declared war on Serbia. Russia sided with Serbia, so Germany declared war on Russia. When France allied with Russia, Germany declared war on France. In turn, Great Britain declared war on Germany. Conflicts and alliances spread, and before long, clashes became a global war. Hitler volunteered for the German army. He felt Germany was a worthy cause to fight for.

World at War

World War I lasted from July 28, 1914, to November 11, 1918, and involved nearly all of the world's most powerful nations. Nations divided into two rival alliances: the Entente powers, commonly called the Allies, and the Central powers. The Allies included the United Kingdom, France, and Russia. The United States joined the Allied cause in 1917. Smaller Allied countries included Belgium, Serbia, Italy, Japan, Greece, Romania, and Portugal. The Central Powers consisted of four empires: the German Empire, the Austro-Hungarian Empire, the Ottoman Empire, and the Kingdom of Bulgaria. At the end of the war, the German Empire was the last to sign an armistice and end the war.

Fighting was characterized by trench warfare. The combat line for each side was a series of deep, complex trenches and dugouts built in zigzag fashion. One series of trenches faced the trenches of the opposing forces. The area between was known as "no man's land." A row of coiled barbed wire stretched across the middle of this area. To attack, soldiers had to go over the tops of the trenches and fire from this dangerous area.

More than 70 million troops fought in World War I. More than 15 million of them died, making it one of the deadliest wars in world history.

SENSE OF DESTINY

Eight days after Hitler finished basic training, his company was engaged in battle against English and Belgian soldiers. It was October 1914. Fighting was fierce, and nearly all of Hitler's company was wounded or killed—3,000 of its 3,600 soldiers. Hitler later wrote that he was nearly wounded that day when an enemy bullet passed through the sleeve of his uniform. It was the first of several close calls he would remember about the war.

Repeatedly, as his comrades fell in battle, Hitler was spared. Each incident reinforced his sense of destiny. He believed fate had put him in this world for a particular purpose. On one occasion, Hitler was the only survivor. A few weeks later, Hitler told his fellow soldiers, "You will hear much about me. Just wait until my time comes."[1]

Because Hitler was not a strong soldier, he was assigned as a runner to carry orders between officers and troops in the field. During the first year of battle, Hitler began thinking about how Germany would benefit from the war. He envisioned a country with one type of people—a pure white race.

BLAMING JEWS

For several years, Germany enjoyed success in the war, conquering Luxembourg and taking large areas of France and almost all of Belgium. Millions of soldiers on all sides were wounded, and hundreds

Sole Survivor

Years after becoming the only survivor of an attack during the war, Hitler told a reporter about the experience: "I was eating my dinner in a trench with several comrades. Suddenly a voice seemed to be saying to me, 'Get up and go over there.'. . . I rose at once to my feet and walked twenty yards along the trench. . . . Hardly had I done so when a flash and deafening report came from the part of the trench I had just left. A stray shell had burst over the group in which I had been sitting, and every member of it was killed."[2]

of thousands of lives were lost. Hitler continued to dodge danger and death. He claimed he had a charmed life.

On October 7, 1916, however, during the long and deadly Battle of the Somme in France, Hitler's luck ran out. While he was sitting in a tunnel with other messengers, a shell exploded near the entrance. Hitler was hit in the upper leg and evacuated to a field hospital. Although his injury was not serious, he was taken by train to a military hospital outside Berlin. Two months later, Hitler was released and assigned to a battalion in Munich.

By 1917, Germany's situation looked bleak. The German people were hungry and miserable. Blockades were preventing food and supplies from entering Germany. Germans wanted an end to the war.

While Hitler was in Munich, he witnessed the dire misery of the German people. But he did not

Poisonous Gas

Poisonous gas was first used as a weapon during World War I. In April 1915, at the Second Battle of Ypres, in Belgium, German soldiers released 168 tons (152 metric tonnes) of chlorine gas. In these early days of gas warfare, almost as many German soldiers died from the gas as the British or French they were fighting. Moreover, poisonous clouds were carried by the wind into the farms and rural countryside. Phosgene and mustard gases were also used by various militaries. In October 1918, Hitler fell victim to a mustard gas attack and ended up in a hospital near Berlin until after the war ended.

blame it on the war; he blamed it on the Jewish
people. Wherever Hitler went, he saw Jews and
accused them of plotting Germany's downfall.

GERMAN REVOLT

On November 9, 1918, after four years of
rationing and casualties, the German military
revolted. German soldiers would not obey orders,
sailors took over warships, and munitions factory
workers refused to make artillery and bombs.
German leader Kaiser Wilhelm II fled to the
Netherlands, a neutral country. Revolutionary
groups took over local government. In Berlin,
German politician Philipp Scheidemann stood on
a balcony and pronounced Germany a republic—a
country governed by the people. The takeover
brought an end to the German Empire—the Second
Reich—that had been founded in 1871.

Two days later, Germany signed a truce. World
War I was over. Seven months later, on June 28,
1919, the final peace agreement—the Treaty of
Versailles—was finalized. It was signed by leaders
of the Big Three: Great Britain, France, and the
United States. Germany was not invited to attend the
peace talks.

The treaty required Germany to take full responsibility for causing the war, the so-called War Guilt Clause. Germany was required to pay $33 billion in reparations to cover war damages. The treaty also required Germany to disarm, limit its military personnel and power, and cede land to Poland, Belgium, France, Czechoslovakia, and Denmark.

German leaders thought the treaty was unreasonable and insulting. But Germany had only two choices: sign the treaty or go back to war. Germany signed the treaty. The punishment would cripple the country economically for many years. Germans would become increasingly angry and repeatedly violate the terms of the treaty. They looked for a way out of their dismal circumstances—a strong leader who would give them reason to hope and the courage to change their situation. That person was a soldier who had grand plans for Germany, his adopted homeland. ⌐

"On November 9 [1918] Germany . . . collapsed like a house of cards. All that we had lived for, all that we had bled four long years to maintain, was gone. . . . [T]he world . . . could not believe its eyes when it saw the collapse of this proud and mighty Germany, the terror of her foes."[3]
—*German General Erich Ludendorff*

Corporal Hitler, 1916

The scene in France when news of the signing of the truce ending World War I was announced on November 11, 1918

GIFT OF PERSUASION

When Hitler learned Germany signed a truce on November 11, 1918, the 29-year-old soldier was overcome with emotion, particularly anger. It was impossible for him to sit still. Hitler wept for Germany.

In November, Hitler was discharged from the hospital where he had been recovering following a mustard gas attack. His eyesight nearly fully restored, the dedicated soldier returned to his regiment in Munich and served as a guard for a few months. The German military was in disarray. The men were lazy and had no respect for soldiers who had fought in the trenches. The country was also in turmoil. Hitler approved of some of the new government's social reforms, but he still distrusted it. He felt it was a way in for Communists to take over, just as they had in Russia. Revolutions were erupting throughout the country, and dissidents were being arrested. German citizens were angry, including Hitler. They wanted prosperity and a higher standing—greater power—in the world once again.

Teaching Hate

Hitler's anger toward Jews continued to grow. He blamed Jews for Germany's economic problems and accused them of controlling the government. Hitler saw that the ranks were breaking because of lack of discipline. He began associating with the Free Corps, a group that believed as he did that Germany had much to fear from Communists' influence. He came up with a "program," which he was to deliver to a group as a speech. In this speech, he began attacking the Jews.

Hitler gained a reputation as a persuasive speaker. His audiences grew larger and larger. For the first time in his life, Hitler had found something he could do very well. Hitler also became known as an expert regarding Karl Marx's work "On the Jewish Question." Marx was a German philosopher who later focused on economics and politics. In general, the "Jewish question" involved any issues surrounding the minority status of Jews throughout the world. When the question came up, people turned to Hitler for answers.

As part of his training as a soldier, Hitler took a course sponsored by the military that provided political reeducation for demobilizing soldiers after the Munich uprising of 1919 in which a local group of Communists tried to take over the government. In September 1919, Hitler's military superior, Captain Mayr, received a letter asking for more information on the Jewish question from Adolf Gemlich, a fellow trainee. Because Hitler was so passionate on the subject and had done so well in the reeducation course, Mayr asked him to write a reply. Hitler wrote

Gemlich a long letter in which he denounced Jews and accused them of "sucking the good will of the masses" and knowing "only the majesty of money."[1] He wrote that legal attempts should be made to deprive Jews of certain privileges and concluded that the "final aim must unquestionably be the irrevocable [removal] of the Jews."[2]

ARMY SPY

The German army also put Hitler to work as a spy. His job was to check on about 50 radical groups in Munich and report back about their ideas and activities. One of the groups was the German Workers' Party (GWP), a small organization founded by Anton Drexler. Drexler, a toolmaker for the railroad, wanted to improve conditions for Germany's working class. Membership in the GWP was limited to Germans who could verify the "purity of their blood" for three generations.[3] Members also vowed they would join in the "struggle against . . . Jewry."[4]

Kurt Eisner

Hitler especially spread hatred against Kurt Eisner, Jewish leader of the Social Democratic Party. Eisner had been calling for Bavaria, the southern area of Germany, to break away from German control. On November 8, 1918, Eisner successfully overthrew the Bavarian government and declared it a republic. On February 21, 1919, Eisner was shot in the back and killed on a Munich sidewalk by a known anti-Semite. In 1989, a monument was built to honor Eisner's memory. A steel silhouette of his fallen body is on the Munich sidewalk where he was gunned down.

Drexler's principles for the GWP were based largely on the teachings of Marx. Drexler taught about expanding and strengthening the middle class and getting rid of what he called big capitalism. He also said that "religious teachings contrary to the moral and ethical laws of Germany should not be supported by the state."[5] Drexler wrote down his ideas in a 40-page booklet titled *My Political Awakening*.

On September 12, 1919, Hitler first visited a GWP meeting. The meeting concluded with an open discussion period. Feeling moved, Hitler rose to his feet and spoke for 15 minutes. Drexler, quite impressed with Hitler's speech and logic, said to his secretary, "This one has what it takes, we could use him!"[6] Then, Drexler pressed a copy of *My Political Awakening* into Hitler's hand, said he must read it, and invited him to come back.

Karl Marx

Although a philosopher, Karl Marx is thought of more as a revolutionary. He set the foundation for communism. In his 1848 book, *The Communist Manifesto*, Marx wrote that capitalism would eventually self-destruct and be replaced by socialism. He believed socialism, which promotes shared ownership, would lead to an ideal future, and perhaps lead to pure communism, a classless society.

GWP MEMBER

That night, Hitler returned to his small, dirty room in the barracks. As was often the case, he could not sleep. He put bits of bread and leftovers on

*The ideas of Karl Marx formed the basis of communism,
which Hitler and many other Germans feared.*

the floor and waited for the mice to arrive. He often
passed the sleepless hours watching the little rodents
eat what he left for them.

Still awake at 5:00 a.m., Hitler picked up *My
Political Awakening* and read the entire booklet. He was

fascinated with Drexler's ideas about a new world order and a new political party for people who were unhappy with Germany. In the following days, he forgot about the booklet. Then, he received a postcard from the GWP accepting him as a member and inviting him to a meeting. Hitler did not want to attend; after all, it was illegal for a member of the army to join a political party. But the military ordered him to attend the meeting and join the party. The army needed an informer inside the organization.

Before long, Hitler convinced the GWP to invite the public to its meetings. The next meeting was advertised, but still only seven party members attended. With each gathering, however, the number of attendees increased. Hitler advertised an October meeting in an anti-Semitic newspaper, and 70 people came. When the main speaker was finished, Hitler stepped up to the podium and gave an emotion-packed speech that lasted 30 minutes.

Anti-Semitism

The word *anti-Semitism* was first used in 1879 by German journalist Wilhelm Marr to describe anti-Jewish attitudes being spread by certain political groups in Germany. These groups were trying to eliminate Jews from public life. The term caught on and soon spread to other countries.

Some feel Hitler's anti-Semitic feelings emerged only after Germany was beaten in World War I but that he exaggerated his claims that his conversion occurred earlier to make it seem more authentic and deep-rooted to his followers.

The audience was electrified and gave him thunderous applause.

More than 130 men attended the GWP's next public meeting in November. Four people were scheduled to speak, but the crowd had come to hear Hitler. When some protestors began shouting, Hitler's military thugs immediately attacked them. These scuffles energized Hitler, and his speech rose to emotional heights as he encouraged the crowd to stand up and resist. He appealed to the audience to love Germany and hate Jews.

The Swastika

The swastika is an equilateral cross with bent arms. It dates back more than 3,000 years when it was used as a sacred emblem in Hinduism, Buddhism, and Jainism. In Christianity, it represented a hooked version of the Christian cross. Some cultures have viewed it as a symbol of life, sun, power, strength, and good luck. In the early 1900s, the swastika was a positive symbol used on postcards, coins, and buildings. Until the 1930s, members of the 45th US Infantry Division, also called the Oklahoma Division, had a swastika on their shoulder patch. Hitler once recalled that when he was dragged to church on Sunday, he preoccupied himself by counting the little swastika tiles around the windows. To Hitler, the swastika symbolized movement. During the stagnant Depression era, Hitler wanted his party to give the feeling of movement. The German name for the swastika is *Hakenkreutz*, or "hooked cross."

In 1920, Hitler decided the Nazi Party needed a flag and an insignia. He designed a red and white flag with a black swastika in the center. As the Nazi regime swept violently across Europe, the swastika became a symbol of anti-Semitism, hate, violence, and murder.

The Power of Speech

Hitler believed power was acquired through public speaking. He wrote, "All great, world-shaking events have been brought about, not by written matter, but by the spoken word."[8] He transformed himself into a great speaker to spread his propaganda to thousands of people at a time.

By the end of the year, Hitler and Drexler had completely restructured the GWP from a debating society into a valid political party. Hitler wanted to introduce the party at a large assembly. Flyers and posters were posted all over Munich advertising a gathering on February 24, 1920. When the day arrived, nearly 2,000 people packed the hall. More than half were likely opposed to Hitler's ideas, but Hitler was bolstered by opposition and welcomed any trouble they might cause. When hecklers disagreed with Hitler, his supporters immediately attacked them with whips and rubber clubs and ushered them out.

Hitler gave a lengthy speech. After two and a half hours of talking, the audience responded with deafening applause. He said,

> When I closed the meeting, I was not alone in thinking that now a wolf had been born, destined to burst in upon the herd of seducers of the people.[7]

The wolf—Hitler himself—would continue to grow in power and popularity until he controlled the country and could carry out his attack.

As Hitler became more powerful, his Nazi insignia became prominent
in Germany and other parts of Europe.

Hitler's strength as an orator helped him quickly rise in the Nazi Party's ranks to become its leader.

THE PEOPLE'S HERO

In 1920, 31-year-old Hitler resigned from the army and focused on his political ambitions. By 1921, the GWP had a new name: National Socialist German Workers' Party—Nazi Party, for short. Hitler was the chairman, and many

German people were calling him the *führer*, German for "leader."

Some believed Hitler was destined to be Germany's savior. In October 1923, after Hitler's rousing hypnotic speech in Nuremberg, one of his followers wrote home:

> You cannot imagine how silent it becomes as soon as this man speaks. Sometimes it almost seems to me as if Hitler used a magic charm in order to win the unconditional confidence of old and young alike.[1]

More and more Germans were sharing Hitler's dream to restore Germany as a respected world power. Hitler was convinced Germans were ready for revolution. He organized a rally in Munich.

THE BEER HALL PUTSCH

On November 8, 1923, 3,000 people jammed into a Munich beer hall to hear Hitler speak. But the rally was not for speeches; it was to announce a putsch, a blatant government takeover. Hitler's private army, the *Sturm Abteilung* (SA), or Storm Section, went into action. Fully armed and marked with swastika armbands, these Brownshirts, as they were called, chanted, "Heil Hitler!" ("Hail Hitler") and Hitler raised his pistol and climbed onto a chair. "Quiet!" he yelled as he shot a bullet into the ceiling. "The national revolution has broken out!"[2] An ecstatic Hitler forced his way to the podium and delivered what some called "an oratorical masterpiece."[3] He said,

> I am going to fulfill the vow I made to myself five years ago when I was a blind cripple in the military hospital—to know neither rest nor peace until . . . on the ruins of the wretched Germany of today there should have arisen once more a Germany of power and greatness, of freedom and splendor.[4]

The crowd roared and broke into song. They sang "Deutschland über Alles," or "Germany above All."

But the meeting fell apart quickly. It was disorganized and rushed, which is why the event is referred to derogatorily as the Beer Hall Putsch. The people sat around all night trying to grab power but could not. They tried to take over the army barracks, but the soldiers would not give up. So, they decided to demonstrate in the streets the next day.

MUNICH UPRISING

At 11:00 a.m. on November 9, Hitler and 3,000 Nazis marched into Munich's central square. They were met by 125 armed policemen. Shots were fired by both sides. Three police officers and 16 Nazis were killed. Hitler suffered a dislocated shoulder and found himself in the middle of the crossfire. His bodyguard, Ulrich Graf, threw himself on the führer. Graf was shot several times, saving Hitler's life. Hitler fled in a waiting car and went into hiding in a friend's attic. Three days later, he was found and arrested for treason.

Hitler was taken to Landsberg Prison, about 40 miles (64 km)

The Prison Guard

While Hitler was in Landsberg Prison, he joined other inmates in the common room. The prison warden, Franz Hemmrich, regularly eavesdropped on the get-togethers. It was his job to find out what they were plotting. However, Hemmrich became captivated by what Hitler was saying. The warden admitted he had an intense interest in Nazi ideology. "Hitler's way of putting things was not mere talking," Hemmrich said. "He made you feel the point come right home; you yourself *experienced* every word."[5] Hemmrich and his assistants regularly listened outside the door to the common room. "[We were] all ears, alert for what he was saying about things that concerned our own interests. We were immensely struck by his speaking."[6]

At the end of each get-together, Hitler said, "Sieg Heil!" German for "hail victory." Then the men would burst into a rousing revised version of a song that had been sung on the day of the Beer Hall Putsch:

Even if they betrayed us
Or herded us like mistreated animals,
We knew what we were doing,
And remained true to the Fatherland.
Hitler's spirit in our hearts
Cannot sink,
Cannot sink.
Storm Troop Hitler
Will someday rise again.[7]

west of Munich. His much publicized trial went on for six months and made Hitler famous throughout Germany. He was found guilty of treason and sentenced to five years in prison.

HITLER IN PRISON

When Hitler first went to prison, he refused to eat. Drexler, who visited him at the end of the second week, was shocked at the depressed, thin, pale man he saw. "I found him sitting like a frozen thing at the barred window of his cell."[8] Drexler was able to snap Hitler out of his depression by telling him that his followers would rather die than go on without him. Hitler began eating again and regained his sense of worth.

He read a lot, scouring writings by Friedrich Nietzsche and Karl Marx. And he began writing in a diary. What Hitler wrote in prison would result in his well-known work: *Mein Kampf.* The book was autobiographical but contained many untruths that made him look good. Mostly, it exposed his deep, growing hatred for Jews. He referred to them as rats, parasites, and germs that needed to be exterminated from all Europe. The job of women was to stay home and raise children. He trumpeted his belief

Hitler at cell window in Landsberg Prison

that Germans were a superior race—better than all other people on Earth. In prison, Hitler's political principles took shape, and his worldview became solid. The problem was that the book was written with such self-promoting and egotistical language that hardly anyone read it.

Rise to Power

On December 20, 1924, Hitler got an early release from prison. He had served only 13 months of his five-year sentence. Prison Warden Franz Hemmrich and his staff actually cried when Hitler left. They had all become deeply attached to this man who spouted negative rhetoric and encouraged revolution.

Hitler left prison ready to revive the Nazi Party and create a pure people—the Aryan race. By February 1925, the Nazi Party was functioning again. However, the government had banned Hitler from speaking in public. Hitler met with Heinrich Held, prime minister of Bavaria, and vowed his allegiance to the government. Held must have believed him, because the prime minister lifted the ban and allowed Hitler to give public speeches.

On February 27, 1925, more than 3,000 people jammed into the same Munich beer hall where the Nazi revolution had begun. Another 2,000 waited outside. It was Hitler's first public speech since his release

Reliable Sources

What is known about Hitler and his regime comes from family members, eyewitnesses, journalists, and historians. Much information comes from *Mein Kampf*. However, Hitler told his story the way he wanted to be portrayed, not necessarily the way it was, so the book is not a reliable resource. Many sources must be checked to determine what parts of *Mein Kampf* are even remotely true.

from prison. He spoke for two hours
to the enthusiastic crowd. An angry
Hitler spewed prejudices and called
for death to Jews and Communists.
The Bavarian government stepped in
immediately and again banned Hitler
from speaking in public.

Next, Hitler worked behind
the scenes organizing his youngest
followers. He divided the Nazis into
34 districts and assigned a leader
to each one. Those districts were
divided into smaller, local groups.
He also revived the children's groups he had formed
in 1922.

Few people saw Hitler during the last half of
the 1920s. No one seemed to notice what he was
doing since Germans were enjoying economic
prosperity for the first time since World War I. In
1926, Germany became a member of the League
of Nations, an international status it had wanted
since the end of the war. But in October 1929,
the crash of the US stock market would rock the
world's economy and become the first step toward
the Great Depression, an event that reached far

Release from Prison

Hitler left Landsberg
Prison by car with his
printer, Adolf Müller, and
his official photographer,
Heinrich Hoffmann. A
group of Nazi motorcy-
clists escorted the men
to Hitler's apartment in
Munich. There, neighbors
had covered his table with
food and drink, and loyal
members of the Nazi Party
who had filled his home
with flowers and wreaths
waited outside for the
return of their leader.

beyond the United States. It would devastate Germany and set the stage for a powerful leader to rise up and promise prosperity and salvation for Germans. It was the crisis Hitler needed to pursue his goal of taking charge of his country and leading Germany to greatness. ⌐

Including Germany's Youth

Hitler's rise to power included Germany's youth, which were placed in different groups. The group for boys ages 13 to 18 was called the Hitlerjugend, or "Hitler Youth." The Deutsches Jungvolk, or "German Young People," was for boys ages 10 to 12. Girls ages 14 to 18 were in the Bund Deutscher Mädel, or "League of German Girls." The Jungmädel, or "Young Girls," was for girls ages 10 to 14. They were trained to be good German wives, mothers, and homemakers.

The Hitler Youth wore uniforms and were trained to fight. They were expected to one day be members of the Schutzstaffel (SS), Hitler's elite military unit. The boys were also taught strong anti-Semitic doctrine.

To the Huntington Library
from
G S Patton
April 14 1945

A deluxe edition of Hitler's Mein Kampf

Chapter 7

Hitler dines with Eva Braun.

ABSOLUTE POWER

After the US stock market crashed in 1929, economies worldwide began to suffer. Just as in the United States, factories closed, banks failed, and unemployment skyrocketed in Germany. Hunger became a daily occurrence.

Many Germans lost confidence in their government. More and more Germans joined the Nazi Party with the hope that the party would lead their country to economic recovery. Most historians agree that had it not been for the economic collapse of the Great Depression, the Nazis would likely have disappeared and been forgotten.

Hitler's Personal Life

The Depression did not affect the personal life of 40-year-old Hitler. In 1929, he moved into a large, new, third-floor apartment in Munich.

Hitler was attracted to a pretty girl named Eva Braun. She worked at the Munich studio of his personal photographer, Heinrich Hoffmann. Braun soon wanted more of Hitler's attention and may have tried to get it by attempting suicide twice, in 1932 and 1935. She was unsuccessful both times, and worse, her attempts did not gain her any more of Hitler's attention. They continued to have a relationship, though not in public. Hitler moved Braun into his villa, but she rarely saw him. He occasionally lavished Austrian charm on the women around him, kissing hands and the like, but it always seemed to stop at that.

PRESIDENTIAL CANDIDATE

Meanwhile, Hitler was experiencing professional success. Each time an election was held, Nazi Party candidates received more votes. In 1932, Hitler planned a run for president of Germany, but first he had to become a citizen. He was officially an Austrian. On February 26, 1932, he pledged allegiance to Germany and was granted citizenship.

Hitler campaigned vigorously with the help of Joseph Goebbels, who served as his campaign manager. Goebbels planned elaborate airplane tours and used radio and film to boost Hitler's campaign. In spite of elaborate efforts, Hitler lost the election. But not by much.

Paul von Hindenburg, the 84-year-old incumbent, was reelected president. Hitler pressured Hindenburg to appoint him chancellor, the highest position in Germany, but Hindenburg refused. The next two chancellors were unable to handle Germany's deep economic crisis. By 1933, Hindenburg's aides and some German businessmen tried to convince the old man that Hitler could turn things around.

On January 30, 1933, when the Reichstag, Germany's parliament, could not agree on the

*With Joseph Goebbels at his side, left, Hitler addressed
a Nazi campaign rally in Berlin in April 1932.*

next chancellor, Hindenburg used his legal right
to appoint one: Hitler. Many Germans, especially
Nazis, were ecstatic. That evening, Goebbels
organized a victory march. Disciplined Nazis
carrying torches marched in orderly rows through
Berlin. For hours, they stepped to the beat of loud
drums and thunderous singing of fight songs. They
passed Hindenburg with respect but went into a
fanatical frenzy at the sight of Hitler. Newsreels show
tears streamed down the faces of German citizens.

Many called it the dawn of a new era. That night, Goebbels wrote about the event in his diary, "The German revolution has begun!"[1]

The German Government

After World War I, Germany's government was called the Weimar Republic. Weimar was the city where the great German intellects, including Goethe and Schiller, lived and studied. It had been selected to be where the new constitution was to be written. The Weimar Republic was highly democratic. In fact, that democratic tolerance allowed Hitler to climb to power. But it had at least one unusual feature: The constitution provided for a president and a chancellor to head the government. The president is elected by the people, but it is largely a formal position. The president's most important task is to nominate a candidate to the Reichstag for the chancellorship who actually becomes more important than the president. It is the same in England and Spain, countries with monarchies that are ceremonial and prime ministers who hold positions of great power.

The constitution gave certain powers to the president. He could dissolve the Reichstag, appoint a chancellor if the Reichstag could not agree on one, and pass emergency bills without the Reichstag's consent. Although the Reichstag could overturn those bills by majority vote, the president could always threaten to dissolve the Reichstag if they did. These constitutional provisions set the stage for Hitler to rise to power.

SWIFT CHANGES

At first, Hitler was cautious and polite in cabinet meetings. Then he boldly took every opportunity to make changes and gain control of whatever he could. Few questioned him. Before long, Hitler convinced Hindenburg to use the president's emergency powers granted by the constitution. In a crisis, the president could bypass the Reichstag to change

laws, and adjust people's civil rights
to establish order.

Hitler then pushed through
a ruling that controlled political
meetings and restricted the press. In
February, an arsonist set fire to the
Reichstag building. Hitler blamed
Communists. Although the arsonist
took sole responsibility for the fire
and said he was not a Communist,
Hitler ordered more than 3,000
Communists and social democrats
arrested. To prevent future unrest,
he convinced Hindenburg to strip
citizens of their right to assemble and
their freedom of speech.

Papen's Deal

Hindenburg did not want
Hitler to become chancel-
lor of Germany. He was
adamantly opposed to the
appointment, which was
engineered by Reich Chan-
cellor Franz von Papen,
who made a deal to be
vice chancellor to Hitler.
The government needed
Nazi supporters to stay in
power because the party
had become so popular,
but they also realized that
political leaders needed
to "control" Hitler and his
people. When warned that
he was placing himself in
Hitler's hands, Papen said,
"You are mistaken. We are
hiring him."[2]

Next, Hitler worked to get the Reichstag to pass
the Enabling Act, which would give the cabinet
authority for four years to make laws without the
consent of the Reichstag. The laws would not have to
agree with Germany's constitution. The act, passed
by the Reichstag on March 23, 1933, essentially gave
all power to Hindenburg and Hitler. Since the aging
Hindenburg was withdrawing from the daily affairs
of government, Hitler took over.

Hitler wasted no time eliminating labor unions and shutting down the press. Goebbels was the new propaganda minister and Germans could read only what Goebbels approved. Hitler mobilized his own police force, the Gestapo, which arrested anyone who challenged the government or was even suspected of a crime or revolt. Before long, Germany's prisons were packed. To handle the overflow, the Nazis built large reeducation camps.

Hitler also took advantage of his new power to strengthen Germany's military forces. In so doing, he ignored the Treaty of Versailles that was signed at the end of World War I. The treaty clearly limited the size of Germany's army and navy.

A Measure of Success

A revolution was taking place, but the Germans barely noticed. Rumors spread about arrests and torture, but parades and celebrations distracted the people from those events. They had confidence in Hitler, who now proclaimed the end to their economic crisis. Then, Hitler proposed that Germany become a one-party state—the Nazi Party. One man controlled that party: Hitler. The proposal passed the Reichstag without opposition.

By the middle of 1933, the majority of Germans supported Hitler. Although he was a harsh leader, he was making their lives better. The creation of the world's first superhighways provided new jobs. The nation's infrastructure was improving, and government money was being used for more teachers to teach propaganda. By the end of 1936, every boy and girl at least 10 years old had to join the Hitlerjugend (HJ), or "Hitler Youth," with its brainwashing and uniforms, complete with a knife on the belt. In schools, the HJ could interrupt a teacher.

Ludendorff's Telegram

Support for the Nazis was not universal. Erich Ludendorff was an army officer who was an early Hitler supporter. Ludendorff sent Hindenburg a telegram. It said, "You have delivered up our holy German Fatherland to one of the greatest demagogues of all time. I solemnly prophesy that this accursed man will cast our Reich into the abyss and bring our nation to inconceivable misery. Future generations will damn you in your grave for what you have done."[3]

GATEWAY TO DICTATORSHIP

Hitler had been chancellor only two months when he declared a boycott against Jewish-owned businesses to be held on April 1, 1933. Jews were removed from government positions, restrictions were placed on Jewish lawyers, and the number of Jews in higher education was reduced. Jews were no longer allowed to own radios. It was a small start to Hitler's plan to first marginalize then completely annihilate Jews from German public life.

On August 2, 1934, Hitler's cabinet passed a law that combined the offices of chancellor and president. It would become effective upon the death of the elderly Hindenburg. Only minutes later, the 87-year-old president died. Hitler was now the sole leader of Germany—a dictator—and supreme commander of the military. Soon, many more Germans would act in allegiance to their new leader. The once unknown soldier, a lowly corporal during the Great War only 15 years earlier, had achieved his goal of control over Germany. But this would not be enough. Hitler would continue to focus on eradicating Jews and building the Aryan race. Soon, the world would know who Hitler was.

Hitler Youth

From 1933 to 1936, members of the Hitler Youth increased from 100,000 to 5 million. Sixty percent of Germany's children were members of the Hitler Youth. By the end of 1936, membership in the Hitler Youth was required.

Hitler's determination and passionate speeches helped him become the leader of the country he loved.

„Extrablatt! — Reichskanzler Hitler!"

Wir folgen Hitler, damit Deutschland lebe . . .

Berlin, 30. Januar.

Stettiner Bahnhof! — kurz nach 2 Uhr. Verschiedene Vorortzüge sind gerade angekommen und der Strom der Menschen drängt durch die Türen in den Vorraum. Da plötzlich Heilrufe. Ein Ruf pflanzt sich fort: „Hitler Reichskanzler!" Jeder hat sofort vergessen, warum er eigentlich auf dem Bahnhof war. Die Hast der Großstadt ist für einen Augenblick einer atembeklemmenden Ruhe gewichen. Niemand weiß, wer die Nachricht, daß Hitler Reichskanzler geworden ist, verbreitet hat, aber alles steht in Gruppen zusammen und diskutiert. Plötzlich sind die Leute schon lange Nationalsozialisten. Jeder will mit dem Herzen schon immer dabei gewesen sein, nur das Geschäft, der Beruf usw. haben ihn abgehalten, sich der Bewegung aktiv anzuschließen.

*

Nur wenige Minuten entfernt in der Chausseestraße die Geschäftsstelle des Kreises VI der N.S.D.A.P. Vor dem Stollwerckhaus, in dem sich die Geschäftsstelle befindet, zahlreiche Gruppen. Alles schaut auf die große Fahne am Hause. — „Wollen mal sehen, ob Hitler besser macht als die, die uns seit so schamlos betrogen haben!" — Das ist

Vor dem „Angriff"-Haus in der Wilhelmstraße viel Volk. Gerade wird die neueste Nummer im Fenster ausgehängt, in dem groß das Bild des Führers steht. „Reichskanzler Hitler."

*

Überall in Berlin, auf den Straßen, in den Verkehrsmitteln, auf den Stempelstellen, in den Kontoren und Stuben, nur ein Thema „Adolf Hitler Reichskanzler!" Das was jeder erhofft hatte, endlich ist es Tatsache geworden. Was der Führer selber erkämpft hat, ein Volk für Deutschland marschieren zu lassen, heute ist es Tatsache geworden. Allenthalben der eine Gedanke:

Wir folgen Hitler, damit Deutschland lebe

*

Gauhaus in der Voßstraße. Vor der Tür, wie immer, die S.S.-Wache. Die S.S.

Ein S.A.-Mann berichtet:

„Wir haben gef

A 1933 issue of Völkischer Beobachter ("People's Observer") *reports the formation of the new German cabinet with Hitler as chancellor.*

LIGHTNING WAR

Early in 1936, Hitler ordered his army to march into the Rhineland. This area bordering France and Belgium was under Germany's political control, but it was to remain a demilitarized zone as a result of the Treaty of Versailles. But Hitler

„Extrablatt! — Reichskanzler Hitler!"

Wir folgen Hitler, damit Deutschland lebe . . .

Berlin, 30. Januar.

Stettiner Bahnhof! — kurz nach 2 Uhr. Verschiedene Vorortzüge sind gerade angekommen und der Strom der Menschen drängt durch die Türen in den Vorraum. Da plötzlich Heilrufe. Ein Ruf pflanzt sich fort: „Hitler Reichskanzler!" Jeder hat sofort vergessen, warum er eigentlich auf dem Bahnhof war. Die Hast der Großstadt ist für einen Augenblick einer atembeklemmenden Ruhe gewichen. Niemand weiß, wer die Nachricht, daß Hitler Reichskanzler geworden ist, verbreitet hat, aber alles steht in Gruppen zusammen und diskutiert. Plötzlich sind die Leute schon lange Nationalsozialisten. Jeder will mit dem Herzen schon immer dabei gewesen sein, nur das Geschäft, der Beruf usw. haben ihn abgehalten, sich der Bewegung aktiv anzuschließen.

*

Nur wenige Minuten entfernt in der Chausseestraße die Geschäftsstelle des Kreises VI der N.S.D.A.P. Vor dem Stollwerckhaus, in dem sich die Geschäftsstelle befindet, zahlreiche Gruppen. Alles schaut auf die große Fahne am Hause. — „Wollen mal sehen, ob Hitler besser macht als die, die uns seit so schamlos betrogen haben!" — Das ist

Vor dem „Angriff"-Haus in der Wilhelmstraße viel Volk. Gerade wird die neueste Nummer im Fenster ausgehängt, in dem groß das Bild des Führers steht. „Reichskanzler Hitler."

*

Überall in Berlin, auf den Straßen, in den Verkehrsmitteln, auf den Stempelstellen, in den Kontoren und Stuben, nur ein Thema „Adolf Hitler Reichskanzler!" Das was jeder erhofft hatte, endlich ist es Tatsache geworden. Was der Führer selber erkämpft hat, ein Volk für Deutschland marschieren zu lassen, heute ist es Tatsache geworden. Allenthalben der eine Gedanke:

Wir folgen Hitler, damit Deutschland lebe

*

Gauhaus in der Voßstraße. Vor der Tür, wie immer, die S.S.-Wache. Die S.S.

Ein S.A.-Mann berichtet:

„Wir haben gef

A 1933 issue of Völkischer Beobachter ("People's Observer") *reports the formation of the new German cabinet with Hitler as chancellor.*

LIGHTNING WAR

Early in 1936, Hitler ordered his army to march into the Rhineland. This area bordering France and Belgium was under Germany's political control, but it was to remain a demilitarized zone as a result of the Treaty of Versailles. But Hitler

• 68 •

ignored the treaty, which forbid military occupation of this land. On March 7, 1936, 25,000 German troops quietly crossed the bridge over the Rhine River and occupied the Rhineland. They were anticipating a counterattack by France, but none came. The German public was delirious as Hitler humiliated the hated French and reoccupied the Rhineland without firing a shot.

KRISTALLNACHT

Over the next two years, Hitler took advantage of his power and created policies that discriminated against Jews and other minorities. In October 1938, about 18,000 Jews with Polish citizenship were transported by train to the Polish border. Hitler wanted to rid Germany of the people he detested. The anti-Semitic Polish officials, pleased to be rid of some of their Jews, would not let them back into the country. With nowhere to go, these Jews camped out in tents at the Polish border in freezing weather.

One couple were parents of 17-year-old Herschel Grynszpan, who was in Paris, France, at the time. When the teenager learned his parents had been forced out of their home and stranded in frigid weather, despite the fact that his parents had lived in

Hanover, Germany, since 1914, he was outraged. On November 7, he marched into the German Embassy in Paris and shot the first German diplomat who crossed his path, Third Secretary Ernst vom Rath. Ironically, he was one of the few anti-Nazis in the embassy. Grynszpan was immediately arrested and put in a French prison.

The incident was exactly what Hitler and Goebbels needed to spark violence against Jews in Germany. They wanted the attack to look like a spontaneous citizens' uprising, so they ordered members of the Gestapo, the SS, and the Hitler Youth to dress in civilian clothes.

Hosting the Olympic Games

In August 1936, Berlin hosted the Summer Olympic Games. Several nations, including the United States, discussed boycotting the event to show opposition to Nazi anti-Semitic policies. Hitler ordered a cleanup of Berlin to hide the city's blatant acts of discrimination. Anti-Semitic signs were removed from the streets. Gypsies, known as Roma, were removed from public view and put into concentration camps. Five years later, when the 1936 Olympic Games had long passed, the Gypsies, like the Jews, were murdered in large numbers.

Hitler used the Olympics to promote Nazi Germany and demonstrate what he believed to be the superiority of Aryan athletes. Only Aryans were allowed to compete for Germany. Hitler openly criticized participants of other races, especially athletes of African descent.

On the first day of competition, Hitler shook hands only with German medal winners. The International Olympic Committee insisted Hitler acknowledge every medalist or none at all. Hitler chose to acknowledge none. African-American track and field athlete Jesse Owens won four gold medals, which especially upset Hitler.

On November 9, Goebbels announced at a reception that Rath was dead. He made it clear the Nazi Party should carry out demonstrations against Jews all over Germany. Almost immediately, German Jews were attacked. Police standing nearby were ordered not to interfere. Nearly 300 synagogues were burned, and about 8,000 Jewish businesses were looted and destroyed. Apartments were trashed. Sidewalks and streets glistened with the glass of shattered display windows from Jewish stores. It came to be called Kristallnacht, German for "crystal night," or Night of Broken Glass.

Jews—including women, children, and the elderly—were beaten and brutalized. More than 400 Jews died as a result of that violent night; some committed suicide. Nearly 30,000 Jews were arrested, many shipped to concentration camps. Jews were now desperate to leave Germany. Over the next year, almost 100,000 Jews left the country. The German public

Taking Flight

In 1938 and 1939, when Jews fled Germany, tens of thousands found asylum in the Nether-lands, the United States, Latin America, Palestine, and Japanese-occupied Shanghai, China. Great Britain accepted 10,000 Jewish children as part of the Kindertransport pro-gram but denied refuge to other Jews, and Canada refused all entry. About 85,000 Jews made it to the United States in the late 1930s. While thou-sands escaped the Nazis, thousands more did not.

View of the Reichstag assembly after Hitler's speech in Berlin on January 30, 1937. After becoming chancellor, Hitler quickly went to work on his plan to rid the world of Jews.

had been brought into the conspiracy. Since they participated, they could never say that they did not know what was going on.

In the weeks immediately following Kristallnacht, the Nazis hauled off more Jews to concentration camps called Dachau, Buchenwald, and Sachsenhausen. There, German guards tortured and humiliated the prisoners. Hitler's plan to

dehumanize Jews and remove them from Germany had begun. It was the first step on the path to genocide.

ALLIANCE WITH THE SOVIET UNION

Hitler was determined to extend his power beyond Germany's borders. To do this, he presented his nation as one with military might. Germany's military also appeared larger than it was. Hitler moved military planes from one airfield to another, so foreign leaders who toured the country would see an airfield packed with fighter planes. They assumed every German airfield was full of military might.

Hitler knew he could not take Europe alone. He needed a strong world power on his side. Germany formed an alliance with the Soviet Union on August 23, 1939. Hitler and Joseph Stalin, the powerful Communist Soviet dictator, approved the pact. The two dictators agreed to divide Poland between their two countries. On September 1, Germany invaded Poland with more than 2,000 tanks and 1,000 fighter planes and advanced on Warsaw, the nation's capital. On September 3, Great Britain and France declared war on Germany. Two weeks later, the Soviet Union marched into eastern

Poland. On September 27, Germany's invasion of Poland began World War II.

As soon as Germany invaded Poland, Nazi commanders ordered Polish Jews to leave their homes and go to walled ghettos, where they were cramped, often several families to a room, and guarded closely. Thousands of Jews died from disease and hunger in the filthy, overcrowded ghettos. Life in the ghettos was remarkably civilized considering the starvation and disease there. Schools were open, musicians performed, worship services took place, and families carried on even as the weak fainted or even died among them. However, from time to time, groups of Jews were marched to the railroad station. There, they would be crammed into cattle cars and transported by train to one of Hitler's concentration camps.

BLITZKRIEG

Over the next nine months, Germany moved quickly, occupying

Dachau Concentration Camp

Dachau opened in 1933. Heinrich Himmler described Dachau as "the first concentration camp for political prisoners."[1] Its opening was announced in the newspaper as a new reeducation camp. It was the first concentration camp in Germany, located ten miles (16 km) northwest of Munich. It became the model for other camps. Most Germans knew something was going on, but it became dangerous to probe too much—informants were everywhere. That many people doubtless knew about Dachau may be seen in repeated common rhymes about the camp: "Dear God, make me dumb / That I may not to Dachau come."[2]

Norway, Denmark, Belgium, Luxembourg, the Netherlands, and France. Germany's ability to swiftly break through enemy lines and take a country by surprise was described by journalists as blitzkrieg, or lightning war.

After taking a country, Hitler ordered Jews there to be controlled and confined. He proclaimed that every Jew had to wear a badge at all times that identified him or her as a Jew. The badge was a yellow Star of David with the word *Jude*, which is German for "Jew," in the middle.

As countries caved to the might of the German army, Great Britain resolved to fight Hitler's evil empire. Hitler was surprised that any country would challenge him. After he defeated France in June 1940, he expected Great Britain to beg for mercy. Instead, the British challenged him and his Nazi regime. Britain strengthened its Royal Air Force (RAF), activated radar stations, and established air superiority over the English Channel.

The Battle of Britain

In July 1940, the Luftwaffe—Germany's air force—filled the skies over the English Channel with fighter planes. The Battle of Britain had begun. It

Battle of Dunkirk

In May and June 1940, more than 300,000 British troops were evacuated from English Channel beaches. The Germans had cut off nearly all of the escape routes to the channel, leaving the British Expeditionary Force retreating to harbor and beaches of Dunkirk, France. The harbor became partially blocked by ships sunk by the Germans. Some 800 civilian boats of all types, including motor boats and fishing boats, ferried soldiers off the beach to ships waiting off shore, and sometimes back to Britain. Many were operated by military personnel; some by their owners. The evacuation saved thousands of lives and rallied the British people.

would go on for nearly four months. Hitler's plan was to gain control of the air space over the English Channel so a German fleet could invade Great Britain from the south. Britain was greatly outnumbered. The Luftwaffe had more than 2,000 fighter planes; the RAF had 640. But repeatedly, the British spotted German planes on radar and shot them down. The British waged dogfights and intense aerial battles over the water, flying so many missions that British pilots were often found fast asleep from fatigue even as their planes rolled to a stop upon landing.

In August, the Germans continued bombing RAF airfields. The future of Great Britain hung in the balance. The British responded by bombing Berlin, which in turn caused the Germans to turn their attention away from the RAF, where they were making headway. Instead,

Germany's Luftwaffe began bombing the city of
London. So, the British again bombed Berlin.
Hitler was furious and ordered more bombings.
On September 4, he delivered a speech in which he
vowed to wipe out all British cities if the RAF did not
stop bombing Germany. Three days later, Germany
began bombing London day and night. The RAF
did not stop bombing Germany. By the middle of
October, German casualties were so high that Hitler
postponed the land invasion of Britain. He had
underestimated the British, and Germany would
never march onto British soil.

Turning on Stalin

A few weeks before, on September 27, 1940,
Hitler signed the Tripartite Pact that united
Germany with Japan and Italy. The three nations
agreed that Germany and Italy would establish a "new
order in Europe," while Japan would establish one
in greater East Asia.[3] Germany, Italy, and Japan were
now allies, a coalition known as the Axis powers. The
Axis would be joined later by Hungary, Romania,
Slovakia, Bulgaria, Yugoslavia, and Croatia.

Stalin assumed the Soviet Union was included
in the pact. He considered it a renewal of the old

Herschel Grynszpan

In 1940, nearly two years after Herschel Grynszpan was arrested in Paris for shooting Ernst vom Rath, France turned over Grynszpan to the Germans. He was taken from his Paris cell and shipped to Gestapo Headquarters in Berlin. Grynszpan was charged with high treason, but no trial was ever held. His fate remains unknown, and he was declared legally dead in 1960.

alliance with Hitler. But nine months later, on June 22, 1941, Hitler betrayed Stalin and swiftly invaded the Soviet Union. Stalin and the Soviet people were paralyzed with disbelief. Hitler and the Germans thought victory over the Soviets would be easy, but the Soviets began fighting back long and hard into the winter months. The Germans were not prepared for the cold and lack of food and supplies. Thousands of Germans died that winter from cold, starvation, and disease. Hitler's war against Europe was not going as he had planned. ⌐

A youth prepares to sweep up the broken glass from the window
of a Jewish shop in Berlin, the day after the Kristallnacht rampage.

Hitler, right, speaks with some of his highest ranking officers.

THE WORLD GOES TO WAR

O n June 22, 1941, in a moment that horrified the German public and the world at large, Hitler declared war on the Soviet Union. Meanwhile, the Japanese were on the move to establish a new order across East Asia. First, they

had to destroy the US Navy's fleet in the Pacific to prevent the United States from interfering.

ATTACK ON PEARL HARBOR

In the early morning hours of December 7, 1941, 353 Japanese aircraft took off from six aircraft carriers and headed to the US Naval Base at Pearl Harbor, Hawaii. The unexpected attack caused widespread destruction to US battleships, destroyers, and aircraft. The loss of American lives totaled 2,402. The words "Remember Pearl Harbor" became an emotional rallying cry at the time.

The next day, the United States declared war on Japan. On December 11, Germany and Italy declared war on the United States. Hitler's decision to declare war on the United States is still unexplainable, given the United States' industrial might and Hitler's war against the Soviet Union and Great Britain. But Hitler believed US President Franklin D. Roosevelt was supported by Jews, so he added to his plan the ultimate extermination of Jews in the United States.

STALINGRAD

By spring 1942, the German army had fought its way to the southern Soviet Union. Hitler was

The USS West Virginia *burns in Pearl Harbor. Japan's bombing of the naval base prompted the United States to enter World War II.*

convinced his troops could take the large industrial city of Stalingrad, but the Soviets fought back fiercely. Stalingrad was particularly important to Hitler. He wanted to march on Stalingrad to break into the Soviet Union and get to the Caucasus oil fields. The Germans needed fuel desperately. Taking control of the oil fields would get the Nazis the fuel they needed and allow them to cut off the fuel supply to the Soviets. In addition, defeating the Soviets would allow the Germans to get through to India and join forces with the Japanese coming from the east.

The battle stretched into the cold winter months, and by November, German soldiers were trapped inside Stalingrad. Hitler refused to let his generals surrender until February 2, 1943, after 425,000 German soldiers had been killed and 91,000 taken prisoner. Only 5,000 would survive their brutal imprisonment by the angry Soviets.

Hitler was furious that his army had been defeated. He isolated himself in his East Prussian headquarters and refused to talk about the war. He became unpredictable, easily losing his temper and going into rages. Inside the Third Reich, a resistance movement was brewing to assassinate the führer. Time and again, however, their attempts failed.

On February 15, 1943, Hitler declared a complete mobilization for victory. Goebbels and Hermann Göring, the people Hitler trusted most, went to work. On every train, wall, and window was plastered the slogan "The Wheels Must Turn Only for Victory."[1] Able-bodied men and women were mobilized from Germany's factories and agriculture to fill the ranks, although this further weakened Germany's industrial base. By mid-1943,

Germany, a country of only 65 million people in 1920, was now fighting on nearly a dozen fronts and simply could not accomplish Hitler's goals.

THE FINAL SOLUTION

In a speech on February 18 in Berlin, Goebbels announced Hitler's Final Solution. Goebbels said Jews all over the world were responsible for Germany's humiliating defeat at Stalingrad in early 1943 with the destruction of the entire Sixth Army and more than 90,000 German prisoners in Soviet

---

Winston Churchill

Winston Churchill was perhaps Hitler's greatest challenger. He began warning the world about Hitler in 1932, long before the Nazi leader became chancellor of Germany. But Churchill was not in a position of power then, and his warnings were heeded by few.

The world began taking Churchill seriously after Germany invaded Poland on September 1, 1939. Two days later, he was put in charge of Britain's navy. The following May, he was appointed prime minister. He gave his first speech to the House of Commons on May 14:

You ask, what is our policy? I can say: It is to wage war by sea, land and air, with all our might and with all the strength God can give us; to wage war against a monstrous tyranny, never surpassed in the dark, lamentable catalogue of human crime. That is our policy.

You ask, what is our aim? . . . It is victory, victory at all costs, victory in spite of all terror, victory, however long and hard the road may be; for without victory, there is no survival.[2]

Churchill believed Britain would ultimately be victorious and he did everything he could to ensure victory, and he was successful. World War II provided what were perhaps Churchill's finest hours as a leader.

hands. He promised that Germany would retaliate for the loss at Stalingrad "with the total and radical extermination and elimination of Jewry!"[3] Loud shouts of support and desperation erupted from the bewildered crowd.

European citizens were becoming indifferent to the plight of Jews. It was commonplace to see Jews wearing the yellow Star of David or to have neighbors there one day and gone the next. Most people assumed Jews were being deported to other countries. While there were 15,000 to 20,000 camps and ghettos scattered across Europe, few people knew that Hitler, through Heinrich Himmler, head of the SS, had created six death camps in Poland: Sobibor, Chelmno, Majdanek, Belzec, Treblinka, and Auschwitz.

Trainloads of Jews, sometimes 20 trains a night, arrived at the camps. It was part of a well-oiled process designed to kill them. Jews who arrived at Auschwitz were divided into two groups: one for hard labor and the other for immediate death in the gas chambers. After being examined by a physician who pointed left or right to designate labor or death, the

Problem Solved

In January 1944, Himmler boasted, "I can assure you that the Jewish question has been solved. Six million have been killed."[4]

majority were herded into large warehouses disguised as showers. After being packed into the showers, the doors were slammed shut and prussic acid crystals were vaporized. Everyone inside was dead within an agonizing ten minutes. The Nazis could kill more than 20,000 people in one day with prussic acid, or Zyklon-B, a gas normally used for pest control. Hitler also ordered the elimination of *Lebensunwertes Leben*, or "life unworthy of life." The racial policy of the Third Reich stated that people who were mentally ill or disabled should be sterilized or killed. When disposal of dead bodies became a problem, crematoriums were built to burn them. Flames roared skyward from four industrial furnaces 24 hours a day.

Hitler seemed to be achieving his goal, but Germany would not be able to sustain fighting on so many fronts. It would be only a matter of time before mighty Hitler would face his downfall. ⌐

Mengele's Experiments

Nazi policy justified performing medical experiments on Jews and other undesirables. Dr. Josef Mengele oversaw the experiments at Auschwitz, a death camp in Poland. Mengele liked to experiment on twins. For example, he would inject one twin with a virus, usually deadly. When the twin died, he would murder the other twin to do an autopsy and see the differences in their organs and tissues. He also conducted experiments on eye color, injecting the eyeball of one twin with dye. This was excruciatingly painful and often resulted in complete blindness. An estimated 3,000 twins at Auschwitz were subjected to Mengele's experiments. Only a handful survived.

*Members of the Allied forces inspect a cremating oven
found at a concentration camp.*

US troops move onto a beach on the northern coast of France on June 6, 1944, during the Allied invasion of the Normandy coast.

THE END OF HITLER

ermany had been doing well in 1941, but then resources were overextended and losses occurred more frequently. Over the next two years, from 1942 to 1944, Hitler became more despondent and agitated. He also stepped

up his mass murder of Jews. Meanwhile, Allied pilots bombed Germany's fuel plants, crippling the country's economy. Germany's army was stretched to the limit, and Germans were discouraged. Then, on June 6, 1944, the war had a major turning point when more than 150,000 US, British, and Canadian soldiers and 30,000 vehicles crossed the English Channel and swarmed the beaches of Normandy, France. It would be called D-day.

Over the next few months, the Allies pushed German troops back relentlessly and made their way through France, Belgium, and finally to the German border. At the same time, on the Eastern Front, the Soviet's Red Army was defeating German troops in battle after battle. As the Allies were fighting across France, about 3 million Soviet troops were on the move toward Germany. Within the Third Reich, military leaders who realized the gravity of the situation were trying to assassinate Hitler.

OPERATION VALKYRIE

One of the masterminds behind the assassination attempt at Wolfsschanze by Stauffenberg was Friedrich Olbricht, a German general. There had been several plots to kill Hitler during his rule and all had failed. Now, the war was looking more perilous for Germany. Olbricht and Stauffenberg began devising Operation Valkyrie in 1943.

Olbricht was in charge of completing the coup with a takeover of the army once he got word that Hitler was definitely dead. When Stauffenberg's attempt to kill Hitler at Wolfsschanze failed, Olbricht, Stauffenberg, and other conspirators were killed on July 21, 1944.

The failed attempt on Hitler's life sent the German leader into crazed behavior as he had the perpetrators shot and hanged and their deaths filmed. At the same time, Hitler's health began to deteriorate. As Hitler realized he could no longer trust anyone, he became more depressed. By autumn, he suffered from insomnia, headaches, stomach spasms, and memory loss. He also showed early stages of Parkinson's disease. Hitler babbled about Vienna in 1910 and his early paintings. Often, he lost his temper and suffered anxiety attacks. Hitler's doctors prescribed more and

Gold Fillings and Hair

Before the dead bodies of Jews were cremated at the death camps, their hair was cut off and the gold fillings in their teeth were removed. Everything was shipped to Germany, where the hair was used to make a fabric used for insulation. Gold was melted into gold bars and sent to Swiss banks.

more pain medications. His mistress, Eva Braun, confided to a friend that Hitler had "become so old and somber."[1]

Holding On

Hitler retreated to a compound at Wolfsschanze in East Prussia. On August 25, 1944, the Allies liberated Paris after four years of German occupation. In September, US troops reached German territory. Defeat for Germany was imminent, except to Hitler, who moved imaginary armies on the map tables and dismissed German generals who did not instantly agree with him. A few months later, he vowed an all-out offensive to win the war.

In January 1945, Hitler and his staff moved to a headquarters in Berlin. German troops were retreating on both the Western Front and Eastern Front. Last-ditch efforts such as the Battle of the Bulge succeeded for a time but eventually ended in failure. The ravages of winter were taking their toll on the wounded, war-torn soldiers. On January 27, the Soviets marched through the gates of Auschwitz, and freed 8,000 prisoners in Poland. They were barely alive, barely able to cheer for their liberators.

By March, enemy troops were rapidly advancing on Berlin from the east. Hitler had grown extremely fearful, constantly worried about being betrayed by his own people. He moved into a huge underground bunker below the gardens at his Berlin headquarters. Depending on the outcome of the war, the bunker would be either Hitler's fortress or his tomb.

On April 20, 1945, Hitler celebrated his fifty-sixth birthday in the bunker. He had dinner with Braun and gave his staff permission to leave the bunker.

The Eternal Jew

In 1940, Joseph Goebbels, Nazi minister of propaganda, ordered the production of the propaganda film *Der ewige Jude,* or *The Eternal Jew.* The film, directed by Fritz Hippler and narrated by Harry Giese, compared Jews to rats emerging from a sewer. The narrator stated that as rats are the vermin of the animal kingdom, so Jews are the vermin of the human race. The film included footage of the Nazi occupation of Poland and scenes of dirty, crowded ghettos. The viewer was made to believe Jews normally lived in these filthy conditions.

Scene after scene, violence and cruelty shocked viewers. The film characterized Jews as wandering rats who only liked money and a wild lifestyle. Aryan men were pictured as strong workers with high values. The film blamed Jews for the decline of the economy, music, art, and science. The film concluded with Hitler stating that Jews in Europe needed to be annihilated.

After World War II, Hippler was unapologetic for producing the film. Later in life, while speaking about his greatest regret, Hippler said, "If someone asks me if I could go back in time and do something differently, I would say I would do it exactly the same."[2] The film is banned in Germany except for limited use in college classrooms where the presenter has had formal training in the Holocaust.

By April 27, the Soviet army had completely surrounded Berlin. On April 28, Hitler learned that Himmler was negotiating surrender. On that afternoon, Hitler sent for the mayor of Berlin and announced that he and Braun were to be married. Eight people attended the ceremony. The couple exchanged rings clearly stolen from some nameless victims.

Hitler had written his last will and testament earlier that evening. In it he declared, "My wife and I choose to die in order to escape the shame of overthrow or capitulation. It is our wish that our bodies be burned immediately."[3] In the middle of the afternoon on April 30, Hitler and his new wife went to their suite and sat next to each other on a couch. Braun died first, by swallowing poison. Then, the sound of a gunshot rang throughout the bunker. A staff member opened the door to Hitler's suite and found the couple dead. Hitler had a bullet hole

Hitler's Doctors

At least four doctors and one dentist served as Hitler's personal physicians from 1932 until his death in 1945. Dr. Hanskarl von Hasselbach treated Hitler's general wounds after the bombing at Wolfsschanze. Dr. Erwin Giesing was an ear, nose, and throat specialist brought to the compound to treat Hitler's burst eardrum. Perhaps Hitler's best-known physician was Dr. Theo Morell, who gave Hitler injections of glucose for energy, started him on large doses of vitamins, and treated a skin condition. He was often on call, sitting patiently outside of important meetings to administer drugs as needed.

in his right temple; his pistol lay at this feet.

The two bodies were quickly wrapped in blankets and carried up 25 feet (8 m) of stairs and outside to the gardens. There, they were doused with gasoline and burned beyond recognition, although an autopsy later proved their identities. Others in the bunker either committed suicide or were killed or captured when Soviet troops stormed the bunker.

Germany surrendered unconditionally on May 8, 1945. Hitler's war was over. The nightmare had ended for Europe and about one-third of its Jews who had somehow avoided death. And civilization was left with the memories of a man—Adolf Hitler—who became the symbol of "Man's inhumanity to man" and a reminder that what he did should never happen again.[4]

Getting Rid of Evidence

When German defeat was inevitable, Nazis began destroying evidence of extermination at death camps. They blasted gas chambers and crematoriums and burned buildings. But the Red Cross arrived to find seven tons (6 tonnes) of hair laced with poisonous gas and hundreds of thousands of pieces of clothing, eyeglasses, shoes, and toothbrushes. They also discovered mass graves filled with hundreds of thousands of human bodies.

The Jewish Memorial Gate at the Dachau concentration camp
serves as a reminder of Hitler's atrocities against the Jews.

TIMELINE

1889	1903	1905
Adolf Hitler is born on April 20 at Braunau am Inn, Austria-Hungary.	Hitler's father dies on January 3.	Hitler drops out of school.

1916	1918	1919
Hitler is injured during the war; he is assigned to a battalion in Munich following his recovery.	Germans revolt; Germany collapses and surrenders.	Hitler denounces Jews and encourages Germany to deprive Jews of certain privileges.

1907

Hitler fails
the entrance exam
at the Vienna
Academy of Fine Arts;
his mother dies
on December 21.

1910

Hitler moves into
a homeless shelter.
He paints and sells
postcards to make
a living. He starts
to form his hatred
for Jews.

1914

World War I begins;
Hitler volunteers
for the German army.

1920

Hitler resigns from
the German army.
He helps establish the
Nazi Party.

1921

Hitler becomes
chairman of the
Nazi Party.

1923

On November 9,
Hitler leads
an uprising in
Munich; he is later
arrested, tried, and
imprisoned.

TIMELINE

1924	1925	1932
Hitler begins writing *Mein Kampf.* He is released from prison.	Hitler revives the Nazi Party.	On February 26, Hitler is granted German citizenship.

1939	1940	1941
Germany invades Poland; World War II begins.	Germany invades Denmark, the Netherlands, Belgium, Luxembourg, Norway, and France and attacks England.	The United States enters the war. Germany declares war on the United States.

1933	1934	1936
Hitler is appointed chancellor of Germany and encourages laws that take away individual freedoms.	With the death of President Hindenburg, Hitler becomes the sole leader of Germany.	Hitler orders the German army to occupy the Rhineland.

1943	1944	1945
Hitler increases murders of Jews with poison gas at death camps.	Hitler survives an assassination attempt in July.	Hitler commits suicide on April 30. Germany surrenders unconditionally on May 8.

ESSENTIAL FACTS

DATE OF BIRTH

April 20, 1889

PLACE OF BIRTH

Braunau am Inn, Austria-Hungary

DATE OF DEATH

April 30, 1945

PARENTS

Alois and Klara Hitler

EDUCATION

Attended elementary schools in or near Fischlham, Lambach, and Leonding. He began attending an Austrian Realschule for secondary school before enrolling in a boarding school in Steyr. He dropped out of that school at age 16.

MARRIAGE

Eva Braun (April 28–30, 1945)

CHILDREN

None

Historical Significance

Hitler aspired to a career as a painter but failed twice to be accepted by the prestigious Vienna Academy of Fine Arts. Following his second failure at getting into the Austrian art school in 1908, Hitler lived a desperate life homeless in Vienna. During this time, his dislike for Jewish people began to develop. Hitler went to Germany in 1913. The following year, he volunteered for the Germany army when World War I began. Following the war, Hitler's skill as a public speaker increased and began being noticed. In 1921, at the age of 32, Hitler became chairman of the Nazi Party. In 1933, Hitler was appointed chancellor of Germany by President Paul von Hindenburg. The two men shared leadership of the country. When the president died the following year, Hitler became the sole leader of Germany. Hitler took more and more power and became a dictator. He sparked World War II in 1939 after ordering the invasion of Poland. For the next few years, he ordered the systematic invasion and occupation of European countries and ordered the extermination of approximately 6 million Jews. He caused and lost World War II, which cost untold millions of additional deaths.

Quote

"You have delivered up our holy German Fatherland to one of the greatest demagogues of all time. I solemnly prophesy that this accursed man will cast our Reich into the abyss and bring our nation to inconceivable misery. Future generations will damn you in your grave for what you have done."—*Erich Ludendorff, German general*

GLOSSARY

adjutant
A military staff member who helps a commanding officer with administrative affairs.

armistice
Temporary termination of fighting by mutual consent; a truce.

Aryan
A term used by Nazis to refer to a hypothetical superior race of non-Jewish Germans with blond hair and blue eyes.

boycott
Not doing business with someone as an act of protest.

bunker
Underground fortification often surrounded with concrete for protection.

cede
To surrender possession of, usually by treaty.

crematorium
A furnace used to burn corpses.

dictator
An absolute ruler who has complete control of a country.

disarm
To lay down weapons; to abolish armed forces.

dissident
One who disagrees or dissents.

führer
A leader, especially one who rules with tyranny.

genocide
Organized extermination of an entire group of people.

Gestapo
The secret police of Nazi Germany.

Holocaust
The mass murder of millions of Jews and other minorities by
the Nazis during World War II.

infrastructure
Basic facilities and services needed for the functioning of a
society.

neutral
Not supporting either side in a war.

orator
A skilled public speaker.

propaganda
Organized spread of information for the purpose of
promoting a cause.

Reich
The territory or government of Germany: First Reich (962–
1806), Second Reich (1871–1919), Third Reich (1933–1945).

Reichstag
The legislative body of Germany and the building that houses
the legislative body.

reparations
Following a war, the money a defeated nation pays to other
nations who may have suffered damages.

synagogue
A Jewish house of worship.

Additional Resources

Selected Bibliography

Hitler, Adolf. *Mein Kampf*. Boston: Houghton Mifflin, 1971. Print.

Kershaw, Ian. *Hitler, 1889–1936*. New York: Norton, 1998. Print.

Redles, David. *Hitler's Millennial Reich: Apocalyptic Belief and the Search for Salvation*. New York: NYU Press, 2005. Print.

Speer, Albert. *Inside the Third Reich*. San Rafael, CA: Ishi, 2009. Print.

Victor, George. *Hitler: The Pathology of Evil*. Washington, DC: Brassey's, 1998. Print.

Further Readings

Dufner, Annette. *The Rise of Adolf Hitler*. San Diego, CA: Greenhaven, 2003. Print.

Giblin, James Cross. *The Life and Death of Adolf Hitler*. New York: Clarion, 2002. Print.

Nardo, Don. *Adolf Hitler*. San Diego, CA: Lucent, 2003. Print.

Warren, Andrea. *Surviving Hitler: A Boy in the Nazi Death Camps*. New York: HarperCollins, 2001. Print.

Wiesel, Elie. *Night*. New York: Bantam, 1982. Print.

Web Links

To learn more about Adolf Hitler and the Holocaust, visit ABDO Publishing Company online at **www.abdopublishing.com**. Web sites about Hitler and the Holocaust are featured on our Book Links page. These links are routinely monitored and updated to provide the most current information available.

Places to Visit

Holocaust Memorial
1933–1945 Meridian Avenue, Miami Beach, FL 33139
305-538-1663
www.holocaustmmb.org
The memorial is a plaza surrounded by black granite panels with a large bronze sculpture at the center that depicts the anguish and death of victims of the Holocaust.

National World War II Memorial
National Mall, Seventeenth Street, Washington, DC
202-619-7222
www.wwiimemorial.com
The memorial honors the 16 million people who served in the US armed forces and the 400,000 who died during World War II. It includes an electronic registry of Americans who contributed to the war effort.

United States Holocaust Memorial Museum
100 Raoul Wallenberg Place SW, Washington, DC 20024-2126
202-488-0400
www.ushmm.org
The museum is a memorial to the Holocaust with exhibits, original artifacts, films, and voice recordings of concentration camp survivors.

Source Notes

Chapter 1. The Wolf's Lair
1. John Toland. *Adolf Hitler*. New York: Doubleday, 1976. 797. Print.
2. Ibid. 799.
3. Ibid.
4. Ibid. 809.
5. Ibid. 811.

Chapter 2. Spoiled and Thrashed
1. Ian Kershaw. *Hitler, 1889–1936: Hubris*. New York: Norton, 1998. 11. Print.
2. Ibid. 13.
3. Ibid. 18.

Chapter 3. Adrift in Vienna
1. Ian Kershaw. *Hitler, 1889–1936: Hubris*. New York: Norton, 1998. 24. Print.
2. Ibid.
3. Adolf Hitler. *Mein Kampf*. Boston, MA: Houghton Mifflin, 1971. 18. Print.
4. Ibid.
5. Ibid. 25.
6. Ian Kershaw. *Hitler, 1889–1936: Hubris*. New York: Norton, 1998. 61. Print.
7. Ibid. 65.

Chapter 4. World War I Soldier
1. John Toland. *Adolf Hitler*. New York: Doubleday, 1976. 64. Print.
2. Ibid.
3. Erich Ludendorff. *Ludendorff's Own Story, August 1914–November 1918: The Great War from the siege of Liege to the Signing of the Armistice as viewed from the Grand Headquarters of the German Army*. New York: Harper, 1919. 429, 431. Print.

Chapter 5. Gift of Persuasion
1. John Toland. *Adolf Hitler*. New York: Doubleday, 1976. 88. Print.
2. Ibid. 88–89.
3. Ibid. 85.
4. Ibid.
5. Ibid. 118.
6. Ibid. 87.
7. Ibid. 98.
8. Adolf Hitler. *Mein Kampf*. Boston, MA: Houghton Mifflin, 1971. 468, 469. Print.

Chapter 6. The People's Hero
1. John Toland. *Adolf Hitler*. New York: Doubleday, 1976. 149. Print.
2. Ibid. 156.
3. Ibid. 157.
4. Ibid. 158.
5. David Redles. *Hitler's Millennial Reich: Apocalyptic Belief and the Search for Salvation*. New York: NYU Press, 2005, 154. Print.
6. John Toland. *Adolf Hitler*. New York: Doubleday, 1976. 198. Print.
7. Ibid. 198.
8. Ibid. 182.

Chapter 7. Absolute Power
1. John Toland. *Adolf Hitler*. New York: Doubleday, 1976. 292. Print.
2. Ibid. 421.
3. Ian Kershaw. *Hitler, 1889–1936: Hubris*. New York: Norton, 1998. 427. Print.

Source Notes Continued

Chapter 8. Lightning War

1. "Dachau." *USHMM.org*. United States Memorial Holocaust Museum, 1 Apr. 2010. Web. 19 Sept. 2010.

2. Morris Janowitz. "German Reactions to Nazi Atrocities." Sept. 1946. *The American Journal of Sociology*, 52(2): 141. Print.

3. John Toland. *Adolf Hitler*. New York: Doubleday, 1976. 634. Print.

Chapter 9. The World Goes to War

1. John Toland. *Adolf Hitler*. New York: Doubleday, 1976. 734. Print.

2. Winston Churchill. "Famous Quotations and Stories: 'Blood, Toil, Tears and Sweat.'" *WinstonChurchill.org*. The Churchill Centre, n.d. Web. 19 Sept. 2010.

3. John Toland. *Adolf Hitler*. New York: Doubleday, 1976. 735. Print.

4. Ibid. 772.

Chapter 10. The End of Hitler

1. John Toland. *Adolf Hitler*. New York: Doubleday, 1976. 778. Print.

2. Adam Tanner. "Nazi hate film maker looks back with some regrets." *David Irving's Action Report On-line*. Reuters, 2000. Web. 19 Sept. 2010.

3. John Toland. *Adolf Hitler*. New York: Doubleday, 1976. 883. Print.

4. Robert Burns. "Man Was Made to Mourn: A Dirge." *RobertBurns.org*. n.d. Web. 9 Aug. 2010.

INDEX

INDEX CONTINUED

ABOUT THE AUTHOR

Sue Vander Hook has been writing books for 20 years. Although her writing career began with several nonfiction books for adults, Sue's main focus is nonfiction books for children and young adults. She especially enjoys writing about historical events and biographies of people who made a difference. Her published works include a high school curriculum and series on disease, technology, and sports. Sue lives with her family in Mankato, Minnesota.

PHOTO CREDITS

AP Images, cover, 3, 6, 21, 37, 38, 47, 48, 61, 67, 68, 72, 80, 88, 96, 97, 99; Gero Breloer/AP Images, 11, 13; iStockphoto, 14; Peeter Viisimaa/iStockphoto, 22; Hedda Gjerpen/iStockphoto, 29; Björn Kindler/iStockphoto, 30; Kurt Strumpf/AP Images, 43; Getty Images, 53, 98 (top); Huntington Library/AP Images, 57; Eva Braun's Album, HO/AP Images, 58; FILE/AP Images, 79; U.S. Navy/AP Images, 82, 98 (bottom); US Army Signal Corps-HO/AP Images, 87; JVT/iStockphoto, 95